The Fireside Book

A picture and a poem
for every mood
chosen by

David Hope

Printed and Published by
D. C. THOMSON & CO., LTD.,
185 Fleet Street, London EC4A 2HS.

ISBN 0-85116-524-9

WINTER LONGING

TO lie in Summer-drenched retreat,
    With rose-crowned archway, and a s
Beneath a singing willow, dropping
Sprays of darkly-golden shadow,
Where tangled woodbine arch a halo
O'er the marble angel dreaming
By the ivy wall a-whispering,
Summer sweet.

Where fiery pokers hot-red dart,
And golden lilies weave their art
O'er trellises; and wild, white twin
Of clematis snows Summer bright.
Then, in that fragrant hour of light,
Summer loving will begin
The melting of the snow within
The Winter heart.

Eileen Melrose

FOR TANGELLO

SHE romps like a puppy, and stands on her head,
   Or occupies most of her mistress's bed,
And wags her ridiculous stump of a tail
To claim our attention — she knows it can't fail!

She loves to recline on a drawing-room chair,
Or lie on her back with her legs in the air;
She knows with a look she can always disarm
Our wrath, with her quite irresistible charm.

With ears wildly flying, and, deaf to our call,
She'll vanish for hours and hear nothing at all;
Then appear, lolling tongue, to dispel all our fears,
Just smothered in mud, full of burrs in her ears.

O little Tangello, you know you can win
Forgiveness for every conceivable sin;
For who could resist the reproach in your look
If for some misdemeanour we bring you to book?

Your soulful expression can plead for our touch,
And if you weren't there we should miss you so much.
I don't think you ever have been really bad;
If you went, then our world would be lonely and sad.

Yes, little Tangello, we owe you a debt:
On the darkest of days you can make us forget
Our cares; and I'm sure that your heart is of gold;
It will always be gay — and can never grow old.

Iris M. Raikes

QUIET, PLEASE!

FULL four and twenty times the 'phone
   Brrr-brrrs before it dies from "No reply!"
The baker's whistle has a knife-edge tone,
And milkmen clang their wire-meshed wares
     nearby.
Towards his cart the thwarted dustman clumps
Because the side door's locked. The parcel post
Rings thrice, then in the porch his burden dumps.

Close on the chime of noon the lunch-time host
Of children heads for home, their passing-by
Announced with yells and shrieks. That scuffling
     sound
Must be the gas man at the meter. Why
Do all these bells and bangs and bumps abound
When I'm in bed with 'flu — and never stop
Right from the time my wife goes out to shop?

Noel Scott

SONG FOR A MIGRANT

COLD, cold the winds do blow.
    High on the hill is the cuckoo snow —
The cuckoo snow that lies till May —
And I heard the cuckoo yesterday.

And when the cuckoo snow is gone
The calving snow may linger on;
And the hill will thrill to the cuckoo's tune
And the calving snow that lies till June.

And in July it well may be
The snow will go, and so will he;
For the Highland Summer's nearly done
When the hills are turning from the sun.

But after blizzard and storm and rain
You may be sure he'll come again:
To the shining mountains and the windy sky
He'll come again, and so will I —
Because we cannot stay away
From the cuckoo snow that lies till May.

Audrey Field

A COUNTRY SONG

GO where buttercups are gleaming
   In the meadow, green and cool.
Go where every leaf is dreaming,
   O'er the shadowed woodland pool.

Go where windmill sails are flying
   On a hillside, while the corn
Ripples to a soft wind sighing
   As another day is born.

Go where little roads are calling,
   And the hawthorn's snowed with May.
Linger till the twilight falling
   Sweetly ends a perfect day.

Peter Cliffe

THE TWILIGHT WOOD

DEEPEST green
   Is the cavernous wood,
Washed in a blue-green,
Sea-green flood;
And deep in the heart
Of the deep dark green,
The silence is heavy
With things unseen.

Step not into
That deep green gloom
Where shadows creep
And the dark shapes loom;
Speak not, tarry not,
Tread not there,
For the twilight wood
Bids the heart beware.

Marion Holden

WHEN I COME HOME

WHEN the long days are over
    And the nights gone by,
And I come home to you, love,
    By the sea will we lie,

By the sea on the cushions
    Of thyme and of thrift,
While the white gulls above us
    On still wings drift.

I'll pluck the small flowers
    To set in your hair;
And the wind will bring the sea's smel
    To us lying there.

And the wind will bring the rumble
  Of stones on the shore:
There'll be joy in your eyes then
  It's long since I saw.

And you'll be in my arms, love,
  Lying close by me;
And we'll not see the gulls' wings,
  And we'll not hear the sea.

John Buxton

STONE WALL

FOR monument of native skill
   In timeless texture living still,
For austere beauty, slowly grown,
Give me a wall of quarried stone.

A wall of Cotswold stone, I mean,
With toppers set on edge and clean;
Not of the smooth, cemented kind,
But stone, rough-hewn, with small to bind.

One of the walls that trophies bear
Of rusted scythe and worn-out share,
Of clay pipe stem and cattle bone,
Back to the times Napoleon.

A sturdy wall with middle filled,
The kind of wall they used to build
When horse and cart from quarry plied
The white lanes of the countryside.

A wall where truant tom-cats roam,
That hunting weasels know as home;
A wall where man may cool his head,
Or sleep beneath, or lie down dead.

Blaze on my shield, posterity,
A horse, a plough, a headland tree,
A furrow turned and, circling all,
A tidy stretch of dry stone wall!

Frank Mansell

LILAC BLOSSOM

IS there a lovelier sight to see
Than blossom on a lilac tree?

A mass of mauve in sunlit May,
Its pale blooms with the breezes sway.

In foaming blossom, scented, lush,
There hides a warbling mistle-thrush.

High on a branch, with golden bill,
A blackbird sings and sings until

The lilac, shimmering for hours,
Becomes a tree of singing flowers.

Breathe in the fragrance of the Spring,
And hear the boughs of lilac sing!

There is no lovelier sight for me
Than blossom on a lilac tree.

Glynfab John

MEMORIES

O LAND of solitude, can I forget
   How I have watched a sudden sheet of spray
   Leap up triumphant on a stormy day
Above the cliffs, when wintry waves beset
A headland of despair — how I have met
Far inland — wanderers from their native home —
The flying feathers of your ocean foam,
And felt the rushing west wind, salt and wet
With driven mist? But I remember most
How all one night, O melancholy land,
   By lone Liscannor Bay, I could not sleep
   For listening to the voices of the deep —
The tramplings of a never-ending host
Along the desolation of the sand.

Edmond Holmes

THE GRANDFATHER CLOCK

IN my Aunt's farmhouse, tick tock, tick tock,
  The pendulum swung in the old brown clock,
How gold-note-calm and distinct each chime
Up the steep stairway deigned to climb.
Still half-asleep I counted to seven:
Morning again in this holiday heaven.
I quickly rose from the goose-feathered bed
Shaking sleep from both limbs and head,
Heard the cool-coo of the Summer-time dove
Answer the call of his lime-tree-love,
And dressing as fast as I possibly could
Ran down the stairs to the hall and stood
To watch the gold-swing in the grandfather clock
Then hurry to breakfast and country talk.

Still, if I listen, I hear the sound
In the midst of the mad world whirling round,
The pendulum swing — not fast — not slow
That measured my childhood long ago.

Margaret Gillies Brown

THE TRYST

THE moon was full, the air was sweet,
  As I walked out to learn my fate.
I took the lane with flying feet
  And stood beside the old field gate.

I heard the church clock chiming deep,
  And grudged the time that I must wait.
Would Katy her dear promise keep
  And meet me by the old field gate?

'Twas but a year since first I met
  My gentle, kindly, grey-eyed Kate.
She seemed to like me well, and yet
  I trembled by the old field gate . . .

I heard her footsteps ringing clear,
  Her murmur low: " My dear, I'm late!"
With eager hands I drew her near
  The shadow by the old field gate.

A whispered plea to share my life;
  Such stumbling words to supplicate!
And when she said she'd be my wife.
  Oh, heaven was just an old field gate!

Peter Cliffe

FLOWERING CHERRY

OH cherry boughs,
   How soon, how soon
The wind has claimed your fragile blooms
And lifted them towards the skies,
A thousand drifting butterflies.

Light as thoughts,
How frail, how frail.
Already told your glorious tale,
Your moment of perfection past,
Pale snow-breaths lie on Summer grass.

Oh blundering wind,
Don't blow, don't blow,
Let the Autumn hour be slow.
Give time to gather from the tree
A wealth of happy memory.

Eileen Melrose

SISTERS

TWO little sisters old and grey
  Struggling along the crowded way,
With woollen coats over ancient spats
And glasses bright under woolly hats.

  *What thoughts are yours of songs that were
    sung?*
  What thoughts are yours of dreams far-flung?

Two little sisters long, long ago,
Skipping gaily as breezes blow,
With ribboned hair and cotton frocks
And eyes so blue under golden locks.

  What songs were yours the whole day through?
  Did any of your dreams come true?

Sheila Leckey

HEN'S NEST

AMONG the orchard weeds, from every search,
   Snugly and sure, the old hen's nest is made,
Who cackles every morning from her perch
   To tell the servant girl new eggs are laid;
Who lays her washing by, and far and near
   Goes seeking all about from day to day,
And stung with nettles tramples everywhere;
   But still the cackling pullet lays away.
The boy on Sundays goes the stack to pull
   In hope to find her there, but naught is seen,
And takes his hat and thinks to find it full,
   She's laid so long, so many might have been.
But naught is found and all is given o'er
Till the young brood come chirping to the door.

John Clare

MAYFLOWER

BRAIDING the hedge the mayflower plays
  coquette
With passing airs, teasing my nose with scent
So sweetly English. Ever yet
The hawthorn bloom has meant
To me the Spring. No other perfume draws
The girlhood of the year so sweetly out.
And did not others find the mayflower cause
To think of England? When the rout
Of waves urged on the ship that bore
The Pilgrim Fathers, seething past in salty crests,
Did not the vessel's name recall a shore
Leagues from the watery waste; and hedgerows
        dressed
In mayflower, white and pink; a foam
Of flower from still-remembered home?

Noel Scott

JANUARY SUN

THE sun, pale invalid,
    Went out yesterday
For the first walk of his convalescence.
Stepping warily, as in a dream,
He smiled softly to himself
Glad to feel his limbs
Though limp and unreal yet,
Glad to breathe earth, thinking
Nothing at all.
And those who saw him,
Ploughman and hedger,
Old wife and dairymaid,
Rook, elm and weasel,
Pleased with his progress
Nodded and laughed.

But today
It is so cold
That he is not allowed to leave his room.

C. C. Abbott

SLEEPLESS NIGHT

I COULDN'T sleep for happiness last night,
   It drifted always in and out my mind;
My room became a silver sloop by moonlight,
  I sailed forgotten seas, let years unwind.

In silence, underneath my silken quilt
  I visited the half-remembered places;
Fast-flowing thoughts like ever restless silt
   Brought back again the lost and well-loved faces,

And to my questing, quiet and wandering soul,
Appeared a clearer vision of the whole.

Margaret Gillies Brown

THE WANDERER

AN old woman comes down the road, dressed
  In a tattered shawl and a threadbare, rust-
  black skirt,
Latticed with squares of blue. She comes silently
As night comes and the fall comes and as the frost.
I watched her face, but there was nothing;
Only a weariness, a strain of the years
And an age-old living . . . always night
And tomorrow coming; drained of emotion;
Set in a mould by time. I would have tried
To stop her. But she was past my ministrations;
Too tired, too old. So she went by, inevitable,
As day comes and the night comes and as tomorrow
  must.
And where she passed, the age-long, restless road
Lay winding; the dust-grey hedge on either side.

Bryan Cave-Browne-Cave

MERCURY

WE found him hidden in a dusty place
    Beyond King's Road — no more the road of
      kings,
All winged for flight, in swift appealing grace;
While crowding traffic, bent on worldly things,
Cared not at all for that immortal speed,
And of his beck'ning finger took no heed.

His ransom paid, he shook the dust of town
From off his errant feet and sped away,
Then of a sudden softly lighted down
Within a northern garden, on a day
Of April, where the trees and native birds
Welcomed him home in better ways than words.

And now the fume and fret are all forgot:
Poised on his pedestal he may preside
Over his own, his happy garden plot,
Beck'ning his favoured friends to come inside
And see his roses: here, no more distrest,
The servant of the gods has found his rest.

Averil Stewart

OLD THINGS

I LOVE old things:
   Streets of old cities
Crowded with ghosts
And banked with oranges,
Gay scarfs and shawls
That flow like red water.

I love old abbeys
With high, carved portals
And dim, cool corners
Where tired hearts pray:
I join them in the silence
And repair my soul.

I love old inns
Where floors creak eerily
And doors blow open
On windless nights,
And where heavy curtains
Dance a slow waltz.

I love old trees
That lift up their voices
High above the grasses.
They do not sing
At the light wind's bidding:
They chant alone to storms.

I love old men
And old, dear women
Who keep red cheeks
As the snows of winter
Keep the round red berry
Of the winter-green.

Wilson MacDonald

BUTTERCUP'S CALF

IT was not long ago, when, quite leggy and
   small,
A little red calf stood alone in the stall;
And we laughed at the flaps of her wriggling tail
While she buried her nose in the depths of a pail.
Though when mealtimes were near she would
      venture to call,
She was happy and sweet, and no trouble at all;
And if others were pretty, they never were half
So bright and attractive as Buttercup's calf.

But months have rolled on into summer, and now
That trim little heifer is almost a cow;
And she'll make a great name as a milker, maybe;
But she'll always be "little Prunella" to me.

Iris M. Raikes

THE SINGER

THIS island singer fingers deep,
  Touches chords that stir from sleep,
Releases half-remembered things
From secret, old, elusive springs.

This island singer with his art
Brings from an overflowing heart
A longing, love and loneliness,
Shawled in a hint of holiness.

With thrilling timbre in his voice,
Notes rise and fall, and with the choice
Of tune plus wild exuberance,
This tenor makes our spirits dance.

He sings of valley, mountain track,
Of moonlight, lovers, flying wrack,
Of hard and sad things, times of joy,
The memories of an island boy.

Here, while upon the stage he stands,
Holding us in his hollowed hands,
He weaves bright bonds for human kind,
Gives us one heart, one soul, one mind.

Margaret Gillies Brown

RAIN

MISS ANNABEL gazed at the lowering sky
    Through a windowpane wet with rain,
"Why doesn't it pour in the night?"
  She cried, pulling over the blankets again.

Old Meadows, the farmer, arose from his bed
    Exclaiming aloud in dismay,
"So much for my toiling and pains,"
  Quoth he, "So much for my plans to make hay."

But Andy, the gardener, smiled and rubbed
    His hands, in quiet delight,
"In a long, dry Summer a shower
  Of rain is most surely a welcome sight."

Whether gumboots or parasols are the rule,
    What the weather be, day or night,
It goes without saying for some 'twill
  Be wrong; for others just perfectly right!

Mary M. Milne

THE SINGER'S PLEA

WHY do I sing? I know not why, my friend;
   The ancient rivers, rivers of renown,
A royal largess to the sea roll down,
And on those liberal highways nations send
Their tributes to the world — stored corn and wine,
Gold-dust, the wealth of pearls, and orient spar,
And myrrh, and ivory, and cinnabar,
And dyes to make a presence-chamber shine.
But in the woodlands, where the wild-flowers are,
The rivulets, they must have their innocent will,
Who all the Summer hours are singing still;
The birds care for them, and sometimes a star,
And should a tired child rest beside the stream,
Sweet memories would slide into his dream.

Edward Dowden

CALL OF THE EMERALD HILLS

ECHOES of the past are calling,
　Calling, through the mists of time,
Emerald pipes of music, haunting,
　From the hills of mulberry wine.

In stillness, slumbering castles rise
　Whose history through the ages ring,
Legends weave the heathered hills
　Of ancient land and Celtic king.

Flaming sunsets, slipping, sinking,
　Drifts of palest peach and gold,
Bloom of grape on fading hillside,
　Black the pen-lined tops unfold.

Folk songs mystical and yearning,
　Still the heart to stop awhile,
Dream of solitude and splendour
　Of that fair and fabled isle.

Kathryn L. Garrod

SMUGGLERS' CAVE

COME, lads, let's go to Smugglers' Cave
    But we must all be very brave,
For in the rock is carved a face
That casts a spell upon the place.

And in the darkness, trembling, damp,
We will explore with torch and lamp,
To see where smugglers used to hide
Their contraband when 'twas low tide.

But in the silence make no noise,
Since we are only three small boys,
And voices echo in the cave
Where gales like furies often rave.

And while we search, in eerie gloom,
We'll hear the distant breakers boom;
Our hearts will much more quickly beat,
Imagining what we might meet.

Perhaps we'll hear spine-chilling groans,
Or stumble over dead men's bones,
And should we lose our nerve, aghast,
Then, lads, we'll make our exit — fast!

Glynfab John

WEST WIND

ANOTHER day awakes. And who —
   Changing the world — is this?
He comes at whiles, the Winter through,
West Wind! I would not miss
His sudden tryst: the long, the new
Surprises of his kiss.

Vigilant, I make haste to close
With him who comes my way.
I go to meet him as he goes;
I know his note, his lay,
His colour and his morning-rose,
And I confess his day.

My window waits; at dawn I hark
His call; at morn I meet
His haste around the tossing park
And down the softened street;
The gentler light is his: the dark,
The grey — he turns it sweet.

So too, so too do I confess
My poet when he sings.
He rushes on my mortal guess
With his immortal things.
I feel, I know, him. On I press —
He finds me 'twixt his wings.

Alice Meynell

HOW LONG TO MAKE A TREE?

HOW long to make a tree?
　　How many rings
Of strong endurance grow
Round the hard core?
What secrets will it see
Of country lore?
What snowfalls undergo?
How many Springs?

How long to make a man?
How many years
Of battles lost and won
Cling to the bone
Since first his dreaming ran
Towards the sun?
What hurts endured alone?
How many tears?

While time remains, our eyes
Will never see
Oak, or the human heart,
Grown in a day.
Science cannot devise
Or love impart
A quick or easy way
For man or tree.

Audrey Field

THE HORSE

GOD made man with breath and soul,
　　Norman and Dutchman, Swiss and Pole;
Irish and Saxon, Swede and Norse,
And then The Lord God made a horse!

He gave him loyal heart to beat,
And velvet nose and dainty feet;
A silken mane that fairly flew,
Fine legs to gallop Heaven through.

The Lord God smiled when Patrick said
"You've surely made a thoroughbred!"
But then, remembering mortal's birth,
God sighed — and put His horse on earth.

God made man with life and soul,
Arab and Negro, Finn and Pole;
Chinese and Indian, Greek and Norse:
And then — the Lord God made the horse!

Sydney Bell

WINTER

THEY sing of Spring, the poets sing
    Of bleating mead and nested bower,
Of green banks set with violet
    And primrose and the pale windflower.

Ah, who shall blame if not for fame
    But for pure joy the poet born
Loosens his words and smites the chords
    In Spring's glad resurrection morn?

But I would say, here in the grey,
    Wan, sodden month of storms and snows,
A word of praise for sombrer days
    Than Spring's new-fangled gladness knows.

Few sounds are heard of beast or bird;
    The wheeling seagulls scream aloud,
The plovers shrill along the hill,
    And curlews pipe from cloud to cloud.

Sometimes a thrush will break the hush
    Of sunny afternoons with low,
Sad notes which seem to mourn in dream
    The faded Springs of long ago.

But oh! the hues, the lucid blues
  Pearling to green, when Morning flings
Her crimson lights along the heights
  And spreads abroad her golden wings.

And if the woods, their dreamless buds,
  Millions on millions, fast asleep,
Lie lifeless, where in sea or air
  Are spacious purples half so deep?

Ah! Winter thou mayst cloud the brow
  Of giddy spirits, but to me
Thou bringest balm, a soothing calm,
  A fixed and rare felicity.

Latimer McInnes

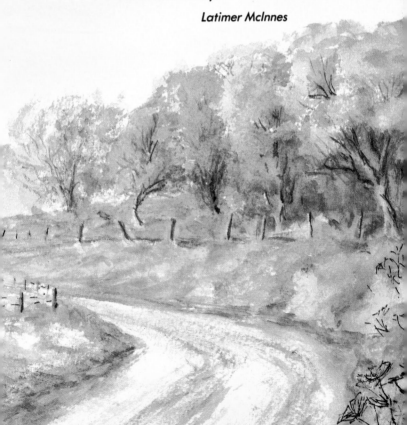

SONG

IF in one crowded hour,
  When life claims every power,
Some vagrant memory draw nigh to touch,
  With fingers hesitant, thy burdened heart,
  Even 'midst the clamour of the jostling mart,
Remember that I loved thee, loved thee much.

  If in one silent hour,
  As dew on thirsty flower
Down falleth softly, over vale and hill,
  Some tender thought upon thy heart doth light,
  Even 'midst the hush unbroken of the night,
Think only that I love thee, love thee still.

Anne MacDonald

SUMMER EASE

DEEP within dappled green and gold,
  Submerged in lucent shades I lie;
Soft meadow grass my ocean bed,
  My zenith the unclouded sky.

So still the waters of this sea
  That scarce a lonely ripple laves
My forehead, or above my head
  Lifts the bright leaves on tiny waves;

This element so light and clear
  That soon my limbs will rise and float
To where the swifts their dark fins sweep
  In circles drowsily remote.

C. C. Abbott

AT SUNSET

THE sun glides down toward the sea
   'Mid amethyst and gold,
    And leaves, at closing of the day,
    Our ship to plough her lonely way
O'er ocean grey and old.

Each eastward mile draws nearer home
And England's sea-girt shore;
    Each throbbing hour of ceaseless time,
    Each bell that peals its passing chime,
A welcome holds in store.

The twilight fades, night's shadows fall.
'Mid stars that gleam on high
    The pale moon climbs with silvery ray.
    Far overhead the Milky Way
Gleams o'er the purple sky.

So speeds the night on westward wings
Till eastern skies grow grey,
    Till Luna fades, and stars grow dim,
    And from the ocean's rose-tipped rim
There flames a new-born day.

C. W. Wade

ARGYLL

THIS is a wild and stormy place:
  The Autumn wind blows keen and chill,
The Ben has hid his frozen face —
  But the bracken shines on the golden hill.

Last night I saw the spindrift whirl
  About the loch with ghostly stride.
Today's an iridescent pearl
  Above a still and dreaming tide.

Sombre and cold the Winter night
  And dusky noon, but I will stay
To read your face without a light
  At midnight on the longest day.

A stranger in this Northern land,
  I think I could not live alone —
But you are there to take my hand,
  And a rainbow springs from the barren stone.

Audrey Field

THE BLACKSMITH'S SONG

LET the fire glow red! Let the anvil ring!
   This is the song that I love to sing,
While the Clydesdales wait in the oak tree's shade,
To be shod anew once the shoes are made.

Oh, iron and man, they belong together,
Let the winds blow chill or in Summer weather.
No job's too big, nor is much too small,
And the sparks fly up at my hammer's fall.

I learned my trade at my father's side;
And he watched me close till I earned his pride.
Now my hands are skilled and my arms are strong;
And I love the forge, though the hours be long.

There must come a time when I work no more,
And the fire grow cold e'er I bar the door;
But who's to say what the years will bring?
So hammer and I, let us toil — and sing!

Peter Cliffe

THE HOMES OF ENGLAND

THE stately homes of England,
　　How beautiful they stand
Amidst their tall ancestral trees,
　　O'er all the pleasant land!
The deer across their greensward bound,
　　Through shade and sunny gleam;
And the swan glides past them with the sound
　　Of some rejoicing stream.

The blessed homes of England!
  How softly on their bowers
Is laid the holy quietness
  That breathes from Sabbath hours!
Solemn, yet sweet, the church-bells chime
  Floats through their woods at morn;
All other sounds, in that still time,
  Of breeze and leaf are born.

The cottage homes of England!
  By thousands on her plains,
They are smiling o'er the silvery brooks,
  And round the hamlet fanes.
Through glowing orchards forth they peep,
  Each from its nook of leaves;
And fearless there the lowly sleep,
  As the bird beneath their eaves.

The free fair homes of England!
  Long, long, in hut and hall,
May hearts of native proof be reared
  To guard each hallowed wall!
And green for ever be the groves,
  And bright the flowery sod,
Where first the child's glad spirit loves
  Its country and its God!

Mrs Hemans

THE MOUNTAINEER

THE searching hand steals slowly up the wall
  And seeing fingers slide around the hold,
While outstretched feet keep balance on the fold:
To hesitate a moment is to fall.
Thus hand o'er hand with foot and back and knee
Up face and crack and chimney, sure and bold,
Till standing on the summit he'll behold
A land of broken rock and jaggy scree,
And gazing o'er mountain, moor and sea:
The surface of a molten earth grown cold,
And breathing air Cuchullain breathed of old,
He tastes the heady wine of victory.
But though he climbs, he conquers not the hill—
It is himself he conquers with his will.

Drummond Henderson

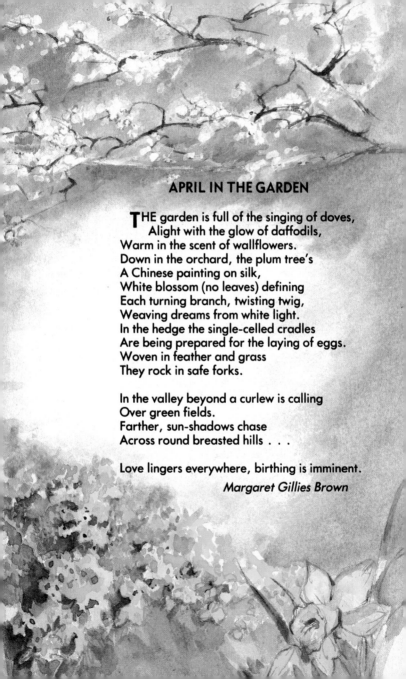

APRIL IN THE GARDEN

THE garden is full of the singing of doves,
    Alight with the glow of daffodils,
Warm in the scent of wallflowers.
Down in the orchard, the plum tree's
A Chinese painting on silk,
White blossom (no leaves) defining
Each turning branch, twisting twig,
Weaving dreams from white light.
In the hedge the single-celled cradles
Are being prepared for the laying of eggs.
Woven in feather and grass
They rock in safe forks.

In the valley beyond a curlew is calling
Over green fields.
Farther, sun-shadows chase
Across round breasted hills . . .

Love lingers everywhere, birthing is imminent.

Margaret Gillies Brown

A PLEA TO TIME

LAY thy hand gently on her brow, O Time,
   Deal tenderly with her;
Around her path the bells of youth still chime,
   The summer breezes stir.

'Tis Autumn, but love's roses bloom today,
   Fragrant as once in June,
And she goes singing down life's shadowed way,
   With heart in perfect tune.

Strange—though the leaves are stripped from
      every bough,
   New buds we see appear,
And, as in Springtime, fill with promise now,
   The twilight of her year.

Lay thy hand gently on her brow, O Time,
   Thou dear and valued friend;
Thou gave her nought but beauty in her prime,
   Give beauty to the end.

Anne MacDonald

THE ECHOING SHELL

HEARD the ocean breaking on the shore,
  A crumbling, sandy sea-beach, and the roar
Of tumbling tides and tossing crests that flew
In scattering foam, snow-white against the blue.
I heard the hiss of the receding waves,
And chuckling pebbles, rounded by the sea,
And echo lingering in the gloomy caves
As music lingers in the memory.

I lost the shell that carried to my ear
The ocean bravely breaking on the beach;
Yet in the silence, intimately dear,
Comes music that no stumbling tongue can teach,
Unless it were in dreaming to invoke
The magic melodies of Tir-nan-Og.

Malcolm K. MacMillan

I WISH...

I WISH I were as chirpy as the birds are every
  morn.
Such incredible high spirits they display!
Though the angry clouds are scowling,
And the vicious winds are howling,
They're up at dawn to whistle cares away.

I wish I were as lively as those feathered friends of
    ours
Out there amid the thunder and the rain.
Though it's snowing, hailing, sleeting,
And their nests must take a beating,
You will never hear them grumble or complain.

I wish I were as tuneful when it's time to rise and
    shine,
And face the hostile world that's waiting there.
Whatever Fate keeps bringing
To annoy us, they keep singing.
It's a lesson they can teach us fair and square.

I wish I were as chirpy as those birds are every
    morn.
They provide us with a message that is strong;
With a whistle and a warble,
All the worries they absorb'll
Simply vanish in an avalanche of song.

J. M. Robertson

B. Glebska

THE TREE

THE tree in Winter's frosty grip,
   Stands tall and dark and bare;
It seems but only yesterday
   A blackbird nested there.

The gentle stream of Summer days,
   That sparkled in the sun,
Now, full-brimmed, hurries to the place
   Where deep dark waters run.

The last sweet rose that bloomed has gone,
   Snatched in a Winter storm,
None but the robin lingers here,
   Alone and so forlorn.

But Winter is the stepping-stone
   That takes us into Spring;
The cherry tree will flower again,
   At dawn the birds will sing.

The golden dancing daffodils,
   And bluebells, will appear,
For God ordained the seasons thus:
   And Spring will soon be here!

Patricia McGavock

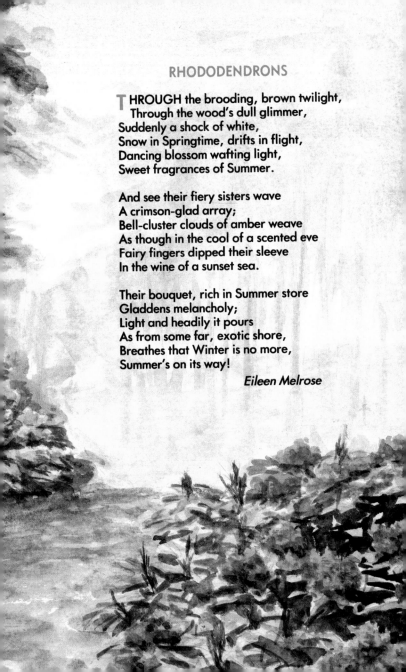

RHODODENDRONS

THROUGH the brooding, brown twilight,
  Through the wood's dull glimmer,
Suddenly a shock of white,
Snow in Springtime, drifts in flight,
Dancing blossom wafting light,
Sweet fragrances of Summer.

And see their fiery sisters wave
A crimson-glad array;
Bell-cluster clouds of amber weave
As though in the cool of a scented eve
Fairy fingers dipped their sleeve
In the wine of a sunset sea.

Their bouquet, rich in Summer store
Gladdens melancholy;
Light and headily it pours
As from some far, exotic shore,
Breathes that Winter is no more,
Summer's on its way!

Eileen Melrose

THE LANDRAIL

I'VE listened, when to school I've gone,
  That craking noise to hear,
And crept and listened on and on
  But ne'er once gotten near;

I've trampled through the meadow grass
  And dreaded to be caught,
And stood and wondered what it was,
  And very often thought

Some fairy thing had lost its way,
  Night's other worlds to find,
And hiding in the grass all day
  Mourned to be left behind;

But I've since found their eggs, forsooth;
  And so we may again,
But great the joy I missed in youth
  As not to find them then;

For when a boy a new nest meets
  Joy gushes to his breast,
Nor would his heart so quickly beat
  Were guineas in the nest.

I've hunted till the day has been
    So vanished that I dare
Not go to school nor yet be seen
    That I was playing there;

So mid the wheat I've made a seat
    Upon an old meer-stone,
And hid, and all my dinner eat,
    Till four o'clock was gone.

John Clare

MY HOME

THE island where I live is like a dream,
   Blue sea, blue sky, and palm trees,
  brilliant green;
Tropical flowers grow in profusion there,
I love their scent and colours rich and rare.
I have a little bungalow, my own,
And yet I cannot think of it as home.
I still dream of a little English lane
And think that I am walking there again.
The scent of honeysuckle is so sweet,
The flowers are blooming all about my feet.
And now I see that little cottage small,
The hollyhocks are growing by the wall,
The old pink rose above the door is there,
Its lovely blossoms scenting all the air.
I see a treasured figure by the door
Wearing the apron that she always wore
And sitting by her side is dear old Shep,
They stand together on the well-worn step.
I can hear well-known voices clear and gay,
My father and my brother at the hay . . .
The dream is fading and I hear once more
The sound of waves upon a foreign shore.
I pray to God that some day I may see
That little cottage that is home to me.

Nora Mathieson

FINAL CHOICE

MARY'S sweet but hard to please;
    Jenny is a little tease.
Sally thinks that love's a bore;
Annabel is so unsure!
Carole used to kiss and tell;
Linda wants to marry well.
But Vivienne is kind and true,
And when she smiles her love shines through.
And Vivienne loves only me,
And she is gentle as can be.
It once was fun to kiss and part,
But Vivienne has won my heart.
I've wooed the others—now and then—
But I shall marry Vivienne.

Peter Cliffe

SUNSET DREAMS

THE world is hushed and the shadows fall
    Soft from the rosy sky;
A sunflush sleeps on the western wall,
    And the sweet bird voices die.

Ah, love, the work of the day is done
    And the evening hour is sweet;
So now when the dawn and the dark are one,
    Ere the pulse of the night's slow feet,

Summon the stars, and the sunlight die
    On the laughing lips of day,
Kiss me and come where the low winds sigh
    To the sunset far away!

Oh come! We will sail to a magic shore
    That our souls have known of old,
In a rainbow skiff from the angels' store,
    O'er the cloud-world ocean's gold;

When wavelets, rosily sunset-kissed,
    Ripple and crisp and curl,
Past isles of Heaven's own amethyst,
    Afloat in a sea of pearl;

Onward, to anchor hand in hand,
    At the cloud-built gate that bars
The golden path to the fairyland
    That lies beyond the stars.

And there I pray we may wander, sweet,
    By the far off mystic sea,
Till the God of the sunset guide our feet
    In the way of Eternity.

Herbert Kennedy

TREES

IN the Garden of Eden, planted by God,
  There were goodly trees in the springing sod,
Trees of beauty and height and grace,
To stand in splendour before His face.
Apple and hickory, ash and pear,
Oak and beech and the tulip rare,
The trembling aspen, the noble pine,
The sweeping elm by the river line;
Trees for the birds to build and sing,
The lilac-tree for a joy in Spring;
Trees to turn at the frosty call
And carpet the ground for their Lord's footfall;
Trees for fruitage and fire and shade,
Trees for the cunning builder's trade;
Wood for the bow, the spear, and the flail,
The keel and the mast of the daring sail;
He made them of every grain and girth
For the use of man in the Garden of Earth.
Then, lest the soul should not lift her eyes
From the gift to the Giver of Paradise,
On the crown of a hill, for all to see,
God planted a scarlet maple-tree.

Bliss Carman

CONSOLATION

O WINTER days are bleak and grey,
And Winter nights are long:
No fireflies where the sedge grows,
No blossoms by the hedgerows,
And in the trees no song.

O Winter days, they end betimes,
The nights fall soon and deep:
Then hey for chair and fender-nook,
The pipe of peace with friend or book,
And long, dark hours of sleep.

Shan Bullock

ACKNOWLEDGEMENTS

We wish to thank Neil Henderson for the use of "The Mountaineer" by Drummond Henderson, and the following for the use of their own poems: Eileen Melrose, Noel Scott, Audrey Field, Peter Cliffe, Marion Holden, Glynfab John, Margaret Gillies Brown, Sheila Leckie, Wilson Macdonald, Mary M. Milne, Kathryn L. Garrod, Sydney Bell, Patricia McGavock and J. M. Robertson.